American Legends: The L...

By Charles River Editors

About Charles River Editors

Charles River Editors was founded by Harvard and MIT alumni to provide superior editing and original writing services, with the expertise to create digital content for publishers across a vast range of subject matter. In addition to providing original digital content for third party publishers, Charles River Editors republishes civilization's greatest literary works, bringing them to a new generation via ebooks.

Introduction

Gene Kelly in *Anchors Aweigh* (1945)

Gene Kelly (1912-1996)

"Fred Astaire represented the aristocracy, I represented the proletariat." – Gene Kelly

A lot of ink has been spilled covering the lives of history's most influential figures, but how much of the forest is lost for the trees? In Charles River Editors' American Legends series, readers can get caught up to speed on the lives of America's most important men and women in the time it takes to finish a commute, while learning interesting facts long forgotten or never known.

When people think of musicals, two of the first names that immediately spring to mind are Gene Kelly and Fred Astaire, two giants of one of Hollywood's most distinctive genres. Without question, both men played an instrumental role in popularizing and sustaining the musical from the 1930s through the 1950s, the final decades of Hollywood's Golden Age. Although they did collaborate on two occasions, in many ways Gene Kelly's rise to popularity in the 1940s amounted to a changing of the guard, because Astaire's career had begun to wane by the mid-1940s. For film historians and fans of the musical, however, even if they weren't contemporaries, Astaire and Kelly will forever be viewed as rivals, with each having left an indelible stamp on the genre that defined their careers. Regardless of which dancer viewers film, there is no denying the cultural significance of some of Kelly's most famous films, including *An American in Paris* (1949) and *Singin' in the Rain* (1952), movies that occupy a central position within the pantheon of Hollywood musicals.

While it is true that a comparison between Astaire and Kelly is indispensible to any study of Kelly's life, much can also be gained simply by focusing mostly on his life and career. What made Kelly unusual for actors of that era is that he did not actually arrive in Hollywood until he was nearly 30 years old, so his early life and work before film had a crucial influence on his star image. Furthermore, given that he came to prominence after Astaire, Kelly's career offers a valuable lens through which to chart the evolution of the musical genre, as well as a look at the prevailing standards of masculinity within Hollywood at the time.

American Legends: The Life of Gene Kelly examines the life and career of one of Hollywood's most iconic dancers, tracing his rise to stardom and the forces within Hollywood and American popular culture that would ultimately lead to the end of his career. Along with pictures of important people, places, and events, you will learn about Kelly like never before, in no time at all.

Chapter 1: Childhood in Pittsburgh

"At 14 I discovered girls. At that time dancing was the only way you could put your arm around the girl. Dancing was courtship." – Gene Kelly

With many film stars, a wide gulf exists between their cultural background and the persona they would later cultivate in Hollywood, but this was not the case with Gene Kelly. Kelly remains famous for his down-to-earth, working class characters, so it is apropos that he was born and raised in a working-class neighborhood in Pittsburgh. Gene was born on August 23, 1912, the third child of Harriet Catherine and James Patrick Joseph Kelly. Gene had an older sister (Joan) and brother (James), and the family later included a younger sister (Louise) and brother (Frank). He was raised Irish-Catholic, though his maternal grandmother was German, hailing from Alsace-Lorraine.

Gene's father James was a salesman for the Columbia Phonograph Company, while his mother Harriet had worked as a stage actress prior to meeting James (Hischak). Appropriately enough, they met in 1905 at a concert in which Harriet performed, and after a very brief courtship, they were married just one year after meeting (Yudkoff). The marriage between Harriet and James was surprising for a couple of reasons. While Harriet was part-Irish herself, being Irish was not necessarily a virtue in her estimation; her Irish father had drank heavily throughout her childhood, and she was also exposed to discrimination against the Irish (Yudkoff). In many ways, James was similar to Harriet's father; since he did not earn much money and was also a heavy drinker.

Harriet was constantly willing to overlook her husband's drinking habits, yet their attitudes toward money and social status were quite different. While James was content to remain a salesman, Harriet was driven toward upward mobility and also spent money more freely (Yudkoff). Furthermore, Harriet possessed a fiery personality, but James was exceptionally laid-back, despite working in a high-pressure profession that demanded he meet a challenging quota of sales each week. Harriet may have yearned for a more prosperous lifestyle, yet there was clearly no possibility for economic advancement in James's career, and anytime the economy stagnated, he would struggle just to make ends meet.

Harriet and James clearly possessed very different personalities, and it should come as no surprise that their differences were apparent in their interactions with the children. As a former actress, Harriet pushed for the children to be groomed for the entertainment industry, so the children took dance lessons, which Gene began when he was just 8. His older siblings resented the lessons, but Gene was more receptive. For Harriet, a life as an entertainer offered the possibility for economic advancement, a sentiment that would eventually prove true for Gene, but shortly after he began taking dance lessons, Gene was ridiculed by the neighborhood boys because dancing was commonly viewed as a female activity. It got so bad that Gene soon quit taking dancing lessons, and he would not resume them until he was 15 years old, as he later recalled, "We didn't like it much and were continually involved in fistfights with the neighborhood boys who called us sissies...I didn't dance again until I was 15." Far from being simply a trivial childhood anecdote, the ridicule Kelly experienced at the hands of the neighborhood kids would influence his later ambitions as an actor, because one of his great contributions as an actor was to demonstrate that dancing and rugged masculinity were not mutually exclusive. In many respects, Kelly's efforts were a response to the harsh treatment he received by his peers during his youth.

As Harriet pushed her children toward dancing, James displayed more interest in athletics, one of the few things in which James showed any competitiveness (Yudkoff). During the week, he was constantly on the road traveling, but his weekends were often spent playing sports with the kids or taking them to professional sporting events. Hockey was a favorite sport of his, and they also attended basketball, football, boxing, and baseball games. From an early age, Gene played a wide variety of sports and was especially talented in hockey, a sport that indulged his penchant for physical contact (Yudkoff). Gene's interest in sports would surprise nobody who saw his muscular frame as a Hollywood actor, but as strong as he would later become, Gene was actually rather small as a child. In fact, biographer Clive Hirschhorn asserted in his biography of Kelly that Gene's love for physical contact developed out of a need to compensate for his small size. Despite his best efforts, however, Kelly was frequently sick or injured. In addition to a bout of pneumonia, two gruesome anecdotes illustrate his daring and the severity of the injuries he dealt with. One time, while sledding, he veered into the street and was brushed by a truck. In another instance, he rode a tricycle without handlebars and fell on his head. This would ultimately prove to be more severe than the sledding accident, as he received stitches and was left with a scar on his cheek that stayed with him his entire life (Yudkoff). As a result of these accidents, Harriet ensured that he would never grow up to be an athlete, and as he reached adolescence, his efforts were increasingly concentrated on dance. As he became a teenager, Gene realized dancing went hand-in-hand with another one of his interests: "I got started dancing because I knew it was one way to meet girls."

Obviously, all the dance lessons would pay off for Kelly in the long run when he rose to fame in Hollywood, but it did not actually take that long for dancing to become lucrative for Gene and his siblings. Throughout his teenage years, he and his siblings formed vaudeville routines, and their performances were so successful that they were booked regularly throughout the 1920s. Gene's younger brother Fred later explained one of their signature performances, in which each sibling would belt out one letter in the family name: "I remember the orchestra cracked up, laughing even at rehearsals. My big sister had the K, my brother James had the E, Gene had the L, my other sister had the other L and then I came in with the Y whenever I felt like it. It wasn't at all with the music; I just took a big breath and yelled Y."

As they grew older, the two eldest siblings grew increasingly disinterested in performing, and frequently Gene performed with just one or two of his siblings. Eventually, it became clear that Gene and his younger brother Fred displayed a remarkable chemistry together, and the two were quite popular during Gene's teenage years. Decades later, Fred would say about Gene, "I'm a great admirer of him. He and I had this great respect for each other. We worked together for 20 years. It's hard to throw that away."

Fred and Gene Kelly

It's impossible to take note of Fred and Gene without comparing their sibling vaudeville act with another more famous one: the partnership between Fred Astaire and his sister Adele. The Astaire siblings grew so popular that they subsidized their family, and although Gene and his brother were not as popular together, it is an interesting fact that the two famous Hollywood dancers began dancing professionally with their siblings.

Chapter 2: An Atypical College Experience at the University of Pittsburgh

"I still find it almost impossible to relax for more than one day at a time." – Gene Kelly

There is no telling how far Gene and his brother Fred might have gone with their burgeoning career, but unfortunately for them, vaudeville began losing its luster as the 1920s progressed. The motion picture industry was steadily gaining popularity, and that increased all the more after the development of synchronized sound in 1928, making it difficult for vaudeville acts to compete. Fortunately for Gene, his mother had long emphasized the importance of education, and he had performed well academically from the beginning, first at St. Raphael Elementary School and later at Peabody High School. Gene graduated from high school in 1929 at just 16 years old, after which he enrolled at Pennsylvania State College with the intention of studying journalism. However, the crash of the stock market that same year precluded continuing his studies, because he had to return home to assist his family financially. Two years later, he resumed his education and enrolled at the University of Pittsburgh, where he majored in economics.

By receiving a college education, Kelly was relatively anomalous amongst movie stars of the era. Jimmy Stewart is perhaps the only star of similar acclaim to have graduated from college, but unlike Stewart, Kelly's family had little money, so he worked throughout his time at Pittsburgh. By the early 1930s, Gene's father experienced had great difficulty as a salesman, and the family responded by opening a dance studio in Squirrel Hill, a neighborhood in Pittsburgh. Perhaps not surprisingly, the dance studio was Harriet's idea according to Gene: "My mother had gotten a job as a receptionist at a dancing school and had the idea that we should open our own dancing school; we did, and it prospered."

In 1932, the name would be changed to the Gene Kelly Studio of the Dance, and initially, the venture was successful enough that a second studio was added in Johnstown, Pennsylvania in 1933. By this time, Gene had become quite proficient in dancing, and he worked as an instructor for his family's Pittsburgh studio. That said, he explained how that was not his goal growing up, noting, "I didn't want to be a dancer. I just did it to work my way through college. But I was always an athlete and gymnast, so it came naturally."

In a sense, it is misleading that Gene majored in economics, because much of his time at the University of Pittsburgh was spent on dance commitments. On campus, Gene joined the Cap and Gown Club, which staged musical productions, and in 1931, the Rodef Shalom synagogue in Pittsburgh offered him a position as a dance instructor. He would continue to work for them for seven years, leading up to his eventual departure to begin his own professional career.

Gene was successful in all of his studies and extracurriculars during his time at Pittsburgh. He maintained a vibrant social life, which included joining the Phi Kappa Theta fraternity, and his theatrical performances with the Cap and Gown Club were popular. After graduating with his Bachelor of Arts degree in 1933, Kelly had plenty of options, and he chose to enroll in the University of Pittsburgh Law School, even though he also accepted the position as director of the Cap and Gown Club, a commitment he maintained for five years. However, while he had been able to balance his studies with his extracurricular activities during his undergraduate years, this became increasingly difficult. Kelly realized that his interests lay in dance, so he quit his law studies after just two months. At this point, he remained with the Cap and Gown Club, but he also concentrated his efforts on performing and teaching at his parent's studio and with the synagogue.

Kelly as a senior in 1933

The success of the family studio and his prolonged involvement with the Cap and Gown Club attest to Gene's skill as a dance instructor, but over time he began to feel disillusioned with dance instruction. The vast majority of students he taught were young women, and Gene's longstanding goal of revising the cultural stereotype of the effeminate male dancer was unfulfilled (Thomas). He later complained, "With time I became disenchanted with teaching because the ratio of girls to boys was more than ten to one, and once the girls reached sixteen the dropout rate was very high." Moreover, his efforts at performing were also stagnant, making it clear that it was difficult to truly achieve success in Pittsburgh. Now in his mid-20s, it became clear that he would need to leave the city in order to find acclaim in the industry, so in 1937,

Kelly finally moved to New York City with the intention of becoming a choreographer.

Chapter 3: Gene Kelly on Broadway

"I'd studied dance in Chicago every summer end taught it all winter, and I was well-rounded. I wasn't worried about getting a job on Broadway. In fact, I got one the first week." – Gene Kelly

While it's easy to understand Kelly's reasons for moving to New York City, his qualifications as a dancer in no way guaranteed employment on Broadway, a notoriously cutthroat industry itself. Although Kelly noted he got a job right away, any potential reservations he may have had were exacerbated when he found out upon his arrival that he had been misled. When Kelly first moved to New York City, he had been under the impression that he was to choreograph a Broadway musical, but this was not the case; in fact, he had only been hired to appear in one dance number (Parish and Pitts). Bitterly disappointed, Kelly returned to Pittsburgh shortly thereafter, and he might have remained a dance instructor in Pittsburgh if not for the efforts of his mother. Undeterred, Harriet still held great ambitions for her children, especially when it came to dancing, and she urged her son to return to New York. At Harriet's insistence, Gene returned in August 1938.

When Kelly moved back to New York City, his expectations were tempered, but he was able to find consistent employment after joining the chorus of Cole Porter's Broadway production *Leave it to Me!* (1938). Gene owed this job to his connection with choreographer Robert Alton, whom he had met years earlier at the Pittsburgh Playhouse. Alton would go on to play an instrumental role in furthering Kelly's Broadway career. Once *Leave it to Me!* concluded, Alton served as choreographer of *One for the Money* (1939), a show that featured Kelly in eight numbers. Also in 1939, Kelly was hired to appear in the musical revue of *One for the Money*, further increasing his exposure. These appearances led to an even more prestigious role in the fall of 1939, when he was cast in *The Time of Your Life*, a production that allowed Kelly to choreograph his own dance routines.

Alton

The remainder of Kelly's time on Broadway was spent balancing choreography with performing. In 1940, he served as choreographer for Billy Rose's *Diamond Horseshoe*, and an even greater break came later that year when he was cast in the starring role of the Rodgers and Hart musical *Pal Joey* (1940). Easily the most significant role of his career to this point, Kelly's performance as Joey, the ambitious young man who dreams of running his own nightclub, drew rave reviews. The show opened on Christmas Day in 1940 and enjoyed a run that included 374 performances. When asked how he managed to dance so magnificently, Kelly told reporters, ""I don't believe in conformity to any school of dancing. I create what the drama and the music demand. While I am a hundred percent for ballet technique, I use only what I can adapt to my own use. I never let technique get in the way of mood or continuity." One of the others working on the production, Van Johnson, credited Kelly's success to his hard work and dedication, explaining, "I watched him rehearsing, and it seemed to me that there was no possible room for improvement. Yet he wasn't satisfied. It was midnight and we had been rehearsing since eight in the morning. I was making my way sleepily down the long flight of stairs when I heard staccato steps coming from the stage...I could see just a single lamp burning. Under it, a figure was dancing...Gene."

Beyond its critical and commercial success, the production is significant in that it included two individuals of great importance to Kelly's career. The first was Robert Alton, who served as choreographer, and the second was Stanley Donen, who would later direct Kelly onscreen, including in *Singin' in the Rain* (1952). As a result of the success of *Pal Joey*, 1940 marks the year in which Kelly's status as a major dancing star was solidified.

Donen

While *Pal Joey* was certainly the more substantial professional achievement, Billy Rose's *Diamond Horseshoe* was particularly significant on a personal level, because it was on the set of the production that he met Betsy Blair, a fellow cast member. The two began dating, and they were married on October 16, 1941. Born in 1923, Betsy was quite young when she met Gene, who was nearly 11 years older than her, but she was still quite experienced as an entertainer, having begun her career as a child actress at the age of 8. One year after getting married, Blair gave birth to a daughter, Kerry, the only child Gene and Betsy would have together, and the marriage remained successful for more than a decade-and-a-half. The couple ultimately divorced in 1957.

Betsy Blair

Gene Kelly's marriage to Betsy Blair neatly corresponded with the close of his time in New York City. By late 1941, Gene had received a slew of offers from Hollywood, but the success of *Pal Joey* made him far from desperate to relocate. Finally, in October of 1941 (the same month as his marriage), he accepted an offer from mega-producer David O. Selznick, one of the most legendary of all Hollywood producers. The offer meant that Kelly would not have to begin his career at the bottom of the Hollywood ladder, as most beginning actors were required to do; instead, he would begin his film career at the top as a headlining dancer and choreographer. Benefitting from the immense success of Fred Astaire and Ginger Rogers' musicals for RKO during the 1930s, the musical was a much-beloved genre at the beginning of the new decade, and there was every reason to expect that Kelly would achieve the same kind of success onscreen that he found on stage.

Selznick

Chapter 4: Western Migration

"I wanted to do new things with dance, adapt it to the motion picture medium." – Gene Kelly

"There is a strange sort of reasoning in Hollywood that musicals are less worthy of Academy consideration than dramas. It's a form of snobbism, the same sort that perpetuates the idea that drama is more deserving of Awards than comedy." – Gene Kelly

Once he had snagged Kelly, Selznick, fresh off his success producing *Gone With the Wind*, arranged for MGM to pay for Kelly's lucrative seven-year deal at $1,000 per week (Parish and Pitts). Thus, while Gene had signed with Selznick, he was effectively a contract player for MGM from the time of his arrival in California. This was by no means a bad thing, since MGM was not only the richest studio of the time but also the one most identified with the musical, and Kelly wasted no time in starring in a major MGM musical, cast alongside Judy Garland in the 1942 big-budget musical *For Me and My Gal*. By this time, Garland had already starred in *The Wizard of Oz* (1939) and was one of the preeminent stars in Hollywood. Having made a name for herself on the strength of her performances as a child actress, she was still in the process of transitioning into more adult roles. On the one hand, her top billing meant that Kelly was not even the principal attraction for most contemporary viewers, but it also meant that the film was not solely dependent on Kelly for its success.

Gene would star with Garland three times in total, and *For Me and My Gal* is the least well-known of the trio, but it was still certainly significant in its own right. Kelly and Garland star as

Harry and Jo, vaudeville performers whose courtship is interrupted when Harry is drafted to fight in World War I. Upon his return, they meet at a performance, and their romance is rekindled. Although the film is set during the previous major war, it is not difficult to locate its patriotic sentiment in the context of 1942, with the romance between Kelly and Garland mirroring that of the men and women whose relationships were interrupted by World War II.

Of course, as with most films of the genre, even more significant than the film's plot were its show-stopping musical numbers. *For Me and My Gal* is interesting in this regard for multiple reasons. First, it was directed by Busby Berkeley, the legendary director who was famous for his lavish, almost kaleidoscopic dance routines, in which the individual performers were indistinguishable and grouped into intricate patterns. However, the musical numbers in *For Me and My Gal* are relatively tame compared with Berkeley's earlier films, and while the movie is something of a novelty in that it offers the possibility to witness a Gene Kelly-Busby Berkeley collaboration, it is far more in line with the style of Kelly's later films than those of Berkeley. To this end, Kelly and Garland are privileged over the other characters, and there is none of the gratuitous camera sequences that define Berkeley's more famous productions.

Berkeley

Despite being Kelly's first film, there are a number of pristine musical numbers, including the title song and "Ballin' the Jack." Keeping with its World War I setting, *For Me and My Gal* is also worth viewing for its collection of that era's songs, including "Where Do We Go From Here, Boys" and "It's a Long Way to Tipperary." Audiences were not only enraptured by Kelly's dancing prowess but also appreciated the way in which the film was able to generate patriotic spirit through its musical numbers. It received an Academy Award nomination for Best Score and was a major commercial success, grossing more than $4 million.

Kelly and Garland in *For Me and My Gal*

Considering the success of *For Me and My Gal*, it would be reasonable to expect that Kelly and Garland would continue to star together, but this was not to be, as their next film together would not come until 1948's *The Pirate*. In retrospect, MGM's decision not to pair Kelly with Garland represents one of the most significant aspects of Kelly's career, because as biographer Rick Altman notes, Kelly never had a consistent co-star the way Astaire had Ginger Rogers. In fact, MGM faced a significant dilemma after Kelly's first film, as they did not quite know what to do with him. When one refers to an actor as being typecast, this typically refers to actors who have limited range and are not stars, but many major actors also rely on an established persona from which they generally do not stray. At this point of Kelly's career, he didn't have a star image, even though MGM was paying him a substantial contract.

MGM's indecision regarding what to do with Gene Kelly is reflected in his roles over the next two years. It may come as some surprise, for example, that his next film after *For Me and My Gal* was *Pilot #5* (1943), a non-musical. If Kelly's first film had been a veiled effort at arousing patriotic sentiment during World War II, Pilot #5 was even more ostentatious in this regard. Kelly plays Vito S. Alessandro, a lawyer serving as a pilot in the war, but the movie was a step down for Kelly, not just because it was not a musical but also because even though it was produced by MGM, it lacked the production values of Kelly's first film. Indeed, *Pilot #5* was an extremely low-budget film that was made quickly and efficiently in an effort to raise support for the war. Later that year, Kelly starred in two other wartime films, one a musical and the other a drama. The drama was *The Cross of Lorraine* (1943), which chronicled the French Resistance.

While 1943 was largely spent on war films, Kelly also managed to star in two musicals that same year, both of which also featured him as co-choreographer. The first of these was *DuBarry Was a Lady*, which also starred Lucille Ball and Red Skelton. The movie was adapted from the play of the same name, although it used comparably few of the play's songs by Cole Porter. Still, the movie contains a number of major numbers, including the title song and "Do I Love You?", the latter performed by Kelly himself. Even more significant than *DuBarry Was a Lady* was Kelly's second musical of 1943, *Thousands Cheer*. Because it is a musical, the film is less realistic than *Pilot #5* or *The Cross of Lorraine*, but it was no less propagandistic. Kelly stars as a soldier who becomes romantically involved with Kathryn (Kathryn Grayson), a famous singer who performs for American troops. The film's patriotism escalates during the second half of the film, in which a wide array of MGM's most famous stars make guest cameos and perform as themselves. *Thousands Cheer* is transparent in its message and is far from a great film on its own merits (although it was nominated for Academy Awards for Cinematography, Score, and Art Direction), but it served to align Kelly with the war effort and furthered his exposure to the public.

In 1944, Kelly again starred in four films, although two of these would not be released until after the year had ended. For the first two movies, *Cover Girl* and *Christmas Holiday*, MGM loaned Kelly to rival studios, a practice that was quite common during the height of the studio era. Just as *For Me and My Gal* had been a vehicle for Judy Garland, *Cover Girl* performed a similar function for Rita Hayworth. Kelly served as co-choreographer and the male lead, but the film was produced by Columbia and Hayworth was the studio's greatest star at the time, so she was clearly the principal attraction. Even though *Cover Girl* is one of the rare films Kelly acted in outside of MGM, it is every bit as impressive; not only do Gene and Rita Hayworth display strong chemistry, but the music features songs by Jerome Kern and Ira Gershwin. A musical comedy, the plot is relatively predictable and features Hayworth as a nightclub performer who becomes romantically attached to her nightclub owner (Kelly). A number of iconic songs highlight the movie, including "The Show Must Go On," "Make Way for Tomorrow," and "Long Ago (and Far Away)."

Kelly and Hayworth in *Cover Girl*

However, the movie was not universally praised by critics, nor was Kelly's performance. Manny Farber of *The New Republic* wrote, "The two things [Kelly] does least well—singing and dancing—are what he is given most consistently to do" (163). This judgment is something of an outlier and may reflect more heavily on Farber as a critic than Kelly as a performer, but it is worth noting that over the next 10 years, the strength of Kelly's dancing effectively eliminated any such responses. What cannot be disputed is that *Cover Girl* was an enormous hit with the public and Kelly's greatest success to date, thus playing an instrumental role in his rise to stardom. Ironically, it took Kelly leaving the studio (at least temporarily) for MGM to fully understand what he could do for them, and how best to utilize him.

After a brief diversion in which he starred in *Christmas Holiday* (1944), a film noir picture for Universal, Kelly starred in the MGM musical *Anchors Aweigh* (1945), his most important film with the studio to date. He again served as co-choreographer but was given the leeway to design his own dance routines. The movie itself is a somewhat bizarre musical comedy that stars Kelly with Frank Sinatra and Kathryn Grayson. Kelly and Sinatra play Joe and Clarence, sailors who take a four-day leave in Hollywood, where they meet Susan (Grayson), an aspiring singer who longs to perform for noted conductor Jose Iturbi. Many other events occur during their stay in

Hollywood, and in the strangest sequence of the film, Kelly performs a dance with Jerry, the cartoon mouse featured in the Tom and Jerry cartoons. By the end, Joe and Clarence are able to find Susan an audition with Iturbi, which proves successful, and Joe and Susan fall in love.

Anchors Aweigh was a remarkably successful film at the box office, and in many ways it laid the groundwork for Kelly's later musicals with MGM. The vast creative control he was given in the film would continue throughout his career, and his dance sequences, which form the core of *Anchors Aweigh*, would do so in his later movies as well. Finally, Steven Cohan locates "homosocial" groupings in many of Kelly's films, and the relationship between Kelly and Sinatra in *Anchors Aweigh* certainly qualifies. Indeed, if the film's primary plotline involves the romance between Kelly and Kathryn Grayson, there is also a deep kinship between Gene and Frank Sinatra that is even more memorable. This pairing performs a valuable function, not only because they maintain great chemistry together but because Kelly's strength (dancing) and Sinatra's (singing) are complementary. Largely on the strength of its musical numbers, *Anchors Aweigh* was showered with award nominations - Gene was nominated for the Academy Award for Best Actor, and the film was nominated for Best Picture and won the Oscar for Best Score. Manny Farber, the same critic who knocked Kelly's singing and dancing, changed his tune after watching this movie, writing, "Kelly is the most exciting dancer to appear in Hollywood movies."

Kelly with Jerry in *Anchors Aweigh*

Kelly's final film of 1944 was *Ziegfield Follies*, which was not released until 1946. As with

Thousands Cheer (1943), the movie was more of a collective effort than a lone vehicle for any one actor, and in fact, Gene appears in just one chapter of the film (titled "The Babbitt and the Bromide"). The most notable aspect of the film is that it paired him with Fred Astaire for the first time, and their number is one of the highlights of both men's careers, benefitting not only from the dancing prowess of the two legends but also exquisite music by George and Ira Gershwin. For two stars used to conducting their own choreography, sharing the screen and dance floor was a potential challenge, but that issue was solved by having Kelly choreograph the first and second sections while Astaire completed the third section. A review of the film in *Newsweek* read, "At least three of the numbers would highlight any review on stage and screen. In A Great Lady has an Interview, Judy Garland, with six leading men, displays an unexpected flair for occupational satire. With Numbers Please Keenan Wynn demonstrates, once again, that he is one of Hollywood's foremost comedians. But the dance act for the archives is The Babbitt and the Bromide...Fred Astaire and Gene Kelly trade taps and double-takes to a photo finish." All in all, even though Kelly appeared in a small role in the film, holding equal ground on the dance floor with Fred Astaire lent additional credibility to his career and reinforced the belief that he was ready to inherit Astaire's position as the top musical star.

Astaire

By the end of 1944, Kelly's career was gaining traction, but near the end of the year, he joined the U.S. Naval Air Service as a lieutenant junior grade. As with so many actors and athletes who enlisted, he did not see any combat but instead served in the Photographic Section in Washington, D.C. (Hirschhorn). His primary duties included writing and directing war documentaries, and it is believed that this played a large role in fostering his interest in producing and directing films (Hirschhorn). As his career progressed, Kelly would assume a more active role in the direction and production of his films, and to this end, his experience serving in World War II actually played a valuable role in furthering his cinematic career.

Gene served in World War II for nearly a year-and-a-half before returning to California in the spring of 1946, and all of the momentum built up during the first three years of his career had essentially dissolved. MGM could not plan around Kelly's return, so they had no project in store for him. As a result, Kelly's first film after returning was the unfortunate *Living in a Big Way* (1947). The plot involves Kelly's romance with Maria McDonald's character, a relationship that is interrupted when he leaves for war. While the film clearly had some contemporary relevance, it was also worth seeing for the way in which it features motifs that would surface throughout Kelly's career. In particular, Kelly dances with a group of children at one point, something that would become a signature of his movies according to Jane Feuer: "When Gene Kelly is not dancing with Cyd Charisse or Leslie Caron, he is likely to be dancing with children…For a movie genre which itself represents professional entertainment and which is also frequently about professional entertainers, there seems to be a remarkable emphasis on the joys of being an amateur" (13). This emphasis on amateurism not only made Kelly more appealing to children but also played an integral role in making Kelly seem more accessible than other stars like Fred Astaire. While Astaire danced in a top hat and black suit, Kelly appeared in plain clothes, with a muscular body that more closely cohered with contemporary standards of masculinity than Astaire's gangly frame. Regardless of which dancer was "better", Kelly would eventually transform the image of the male dancer away from the elitist connotations of Astaire and toward a more virile masculinity that appealed to typical American men.

Living in a Big Way proved to be Kelly's only film in 1947, but he was much busier in 1948. First, he starred in an adaptation of *The Three Musketeers* (1948) as d'Artagnan, but his biggest role came in *The Pirate* (1948), which remains one of the defining achievements of his career. Kelly was reunited with Judy Garland for the film, but by this time, Garland's addiction to prescription drugs had worsened substantially. She would have great difficulty even committing to films over the next 15 years before dying in 1969 at just 45 years old. By the late 1940s, other major stars (Cary Grant chief among them) refused to work with Garland, but Kelly was sympathetic and maintained a genial relationship with the actress. The acclaimed Vincente Minnelli served as director, and as much as *The Pirate* is a vehicle for Kelly, it is also very much a Minnelli film, as evidenced by the film's deft balance between the everyday and the extraordinary. In the movie, Garland stars as Manuela, a young lady who lives in Calvados, a small Caribbean town. Kelly's character, Serafin, yearns to be with Manuela but is rejected by her. To trick her into falling for him, he impersonates the notorious pirate Macoco, nicknamed "Mack the Black", and even though she eventually realizes his true identity, she ultimately falls in love with him anyway.

Kelly in *The Pirate*

Like many of Minnelli's other films, *The Pirate* contains a rather flimsy plot that is enhanced by the sumptuous musical numbers. In that regard, Minnelli, who remains famous for his elaborate set designs and costuming (a skill he had perfected during his earlier job designing shop windows), did a remarkable job with *The Pirate*. Kelly's costume as Macoco is most notable, featuring a tight black outfit (complete with a black bandana) that shows off his muscular frame to full effect. In *The Pirate*, viewers gets a full sense of just how different Gene Kelly was from Fred Astaire; Kelly's action-hero physique is worlds apart from the more delicate physique of Astaire, and his pirate outfit exposes the almost elitist character of Astaire's most famous roles. As famous as Garland still was in 1948, it is Kelly who is objectified more than Garland, which constitutes a clear reversal of the traditional dynamic in which the male character is the surrogate for the viewer to gaze at the female. From the outset of the film, it is clear that Gene Kelly is the star attraction, and the film is a testament to his prowess as the preeminent actor of the musical during the 1940s and early years of the following decade.

Gene Kelly's objectification in *The Pirate* also gestures toward the camp dimension that is central to his star persona. This camp quality also manifests through the homosocial motif discussed with regard to *Anchors Aweigh*, but the costuming in *The Pirate* is perhaps an even better example. A contrast formed between his masculinity and the more feminine connotations that traditionally accompany singing and dancing, and Steven Cohan articulates how this contrast challenged standards of masculinity: "Far from being fixed early on and all of a piece, the Kelly image embodied a provocative disjunction of gendered and sexualized understandings of masculinity, which in turn produced an indecipherable picture of what it meant to dance 'in the right way'. The extra-filmic commentary about Kelly at that time defined the particularities of his star image by focusing on the way his dancing troubled rather than secured masculine norms…Kelly embodied what amounted to a cultural oxymoron, namely, the erotic spectacle of a male dancer, which problematised binary formations of masculinity and heterosexuality. In doing so, this star image established the ground for viewing Kelly's dancing from a camp perspective." (19).

This objectification of the male lead constitutes another break from Fred Astaire. Astaire's famous dances typically feature Ginger Rogers as the figure who is objectified, but in Kelly's films, he is the one who is objectified. This was not only a novel development within the genre but also within Hollywood as a whole, and even though *The Pirate* did not receive the critical praise of other Kelly films, it is perhaps the best example of the changes Kelly brought to the genre, and the representation of masculinity in film.

On the heels of *The Pirate*, it looked as though MGM might capitalize on the film's success and pair Garland and Kelly again. The two were slated to star together in *Easter Parade* (1948), but Gene injured himself while playing volleyball, and though Kelly and Garland would pair up again, it wouldn't be that movie. Instead, Kelly convinced Astaire to return from retirement and star in the film (Astaire). This decision would prove fortuitous for Astaire, who would star in several successful films following the completion of *Easter Parade*.

For his part, Kelly's next starring role was in *Take Me Out to the Ball Game* (1949), a film that was originally supposed to star Garland, but in a theme that would only grow more common, her substance abuse problems forced her to withdraw from the project. As its title suggests, the film revolves around a baseball team; like *Anchors Aweigh*, Kelly stars with Frank Sinatra as two baseball players on a team with a female owner. The decision to cast Kelly as a baseball player is surprising since Kelly stood just 5-feet-7 inches, but he was muscular enough to overcome that. The narrative centers on their attempts to romance the owner, but much of the movie's attraction also derives from the fact that the two characters double as vaudeville performers. With Sinatra and Kelly together, it goes without saying that MGM invested a great deal of money in the film, and it was a tremendous success and one of the most successful musicals of the decade.

Take Me Out to the Ball Game is not as well-known as several of Kelly's other films, but it should not go overlooked in discussions of his career. Similar to *Anchors Aweigh*, a highlight is simply the opportunity to watch him together with Sinatra, who was primarily known for his talents as a solo artist. The actual plot is unremarkable, and it is telling that the musical numbers are better-known than the storyline. A number of famous musical numbers highlight the film, most notably "Take Me Out to the Ballgame." It is telling that the chemistry between Sinatra and Kelly is stronger than the rapport between both actors and Esther Williams, the film's female lead. As such, *Take Me Out to the Ball Game* is another example of the way in which Kelly's films frequently feature an all-male friendship that is more compelling than his relationship with the main actress.

Kelly in the trailer for *Take Me Out to the Ball Game*

Take Me Out to the Ball Game was not the only Gene Kelly film from 1949; and his second film that year, *On the Town* (1949), was nearly as successful. The movie reprised the successful pairing of Kelly and Sinatra, and the plot recalls elements of *Anchors Aweigh*. The two actors star as sailors enjoying their shore leave in New York City, which brings to mind the plot of the previous film, albeit set in New York City. Furthermore, by 1949, Kelly was no longer just an actor and co-choreographer but also assumed primary control over the directorial decisions, with Stanley Donen serving as co-director.

The working relationship between Kelly and Donen would prove critical, because while Fred Astaire had Hermes Pan (who served as choreographer for many of Astaire's films), Gene had Stanley Donen. A close friend of Kelly's, Donen had served as one of the writers for *Take Me Out to the Ball Game*, and he and Kelly formed a close bond and would work together on several occasions. Donen had arrived in Hollywood with the purpose of serving as a co-choreographer to Kelly, but their friendship quickly blossomed, and over time, Donen would become quite adept as a director. Kelly spoke of him in glowing terms: "[W]hen you are involved in doing choreography for film you must have expert assistants. I needed one to watch my performance, and one to work with the cameraman on the timing...I could never have done these things. When we came to do On the Town, I knew it was time for Stanley to get screen credit because we weren't boss-assistant anymore but co-creators" (Thomas 20).

As much credit as Donen deserves, it was just as important that Kelly took such interest in the filmmaking side of his movies. Indeed, Gene's interest in directing, which was first born out of his experiences directing during World War II, is another difference separating him from Fred Astaire. While Fred Astaire maintained creative control over his dance routines, he played no part in the art direction, so as Astaire remained entrenched in the role of musical performer, Kelly expanded on this and qualifies as more of a filmmaker.

No expense was spared with *On the Town*, and it shows, because the movie boasts some of the most impressive production values of any of Kelly's films. Like many MGM musicals, the Technicolor makes for a vibrant aesthetic, and the color earned a Golden Globe nomination. An additional pleasure is that all of the musical numbers in *On the Town* were shot on-location in New York City; while shooting on-location is now hardly uncommon, Stanley Green notes that this was the first time MGM had shot on-location. Going along with the graphics were great songs, which were under the creative control of Leonard Bernstein, and several of the musical numbers, including "New York, New York," "Prehistoric Man," and "Miss Turnstiles Ballet," rank among the most famous of the genre. The movie won the Academy Award for Best Music, but the money spent on the high-profile actors, composers, and production made it difficult for the film to turn a profit; in fact, more than $2 million was spent in total. Fortunately, the film received strong reviews and benefitted greatly from the popularity of its two main stars. It easily grossed more than the production cost and ranks as one of the great achievements of Kelly's career.

All told, the 1940s were the busiest decade of Kelly's career, spanning the tail end of his Broadway career, the earliest years of his Hollywood career, his service in World War II, and several of his defining films in *The Pirate, Take Me Out to the Ball Game,* and *On the Town.* On a personal level, the decade also saw him get married, with he and wife Betsy Blair having their first child as well. Prior to his service in the war, Kelly had yet to solidify his status as a major star, but 1947-1949 comprise arguably the most important years of his career, three years in which his recognition as a god of the musical was solidified. For these reasons, it could be argued that it was the most successful decade for Kelly. The next 10 years would produce mixed results, with some of Kelly's greatest career achievements but also the beginning of the end to his career.

Chapter 5: Gene Kelly in the 1950s

"Gene is easygoing as long as you know exactly what you are doing when you're working with him. He's a hard taskmaster and he loves hard work. If you want to play on his team you'd better like hard work, too. He isn't cruel but he is tough, and if Gene believed in something he didn't care who he was talking to, whether it was Louis B. Mayer or the gatekeeper. He wasn't awed by anybody, and he had a good record of getting what he wanted" – Johnny Green, head of music at MGM

By the time 1950 arrived, Gene Kelly's career could not have been in a better place, and his films from early in the decade are truly memorable. The first of these was *Summer Stock*, which starred him alongside Judy Garland once again. In fact, production for the movie had begun in 1948, yet Judy's ongoing battles with drug addiction frequently stalled the production. As a result, the movie is particularly unusual because scenes from later in the film were shot more than a year after the earlier ones. Garland's erratic behavior effectively ruined her relationship with MGM, the studio that had brought her to prominence as a child star during the 1930s; fed up with her behavior, her contract was terminated following the conclusion of *Summer Stock*, and as a result, the movie stands as the last time Kelly and Garland appeared together onscreen.

Not surprisingly, *Summer Stock* is now somewhat overshadowed by the film's notorious production history, remaining better remembered for Judy Garland's personal struggles and performance in the film than any of the contributions made by Gene Kelly. For example, viewers cannot help but notice that Garland is significantly heavier in the earlier scenes of the film, when her alcoholism had spiraled out of control. From 1948-1949, she sought help and lost 20 pounds by refraining from drinking, and her performance of "Get Happy," which occurs late in the film and shows off her healthier physique, stands as one of the crowning achievements of Garland's career. As for Kelly, three of his musical numbers - "You, Wonderful You," "Portland Fancy," and "(Howdy Neighbor) Happy Harvest" - make the film not only memorable for fans of Judy Garland but also for connoisseurs of the genre.

When Judy Garland split with MGM, Kelly lost the actress with whom he had most frequently collaborated, but this didn't end up hindering his career. In fact, his next two films, *An American in Paris* (1951) and *Singin' in the Rain* (1952), are among the most praiseworthy of his career. In the former, Kelly worked again with Vincente Minnelli (who had directed him in *The Pirate*) and starred with Leslie Caron and Oscar Levant. As usual, MGM brought all of its financial muscle to the production; not only were Kelly, Minnelli, and Caron all major stars, but George and Ira Gershwin composed the music. Altogether, the budget totaled more than $2.7 million, but it still turned a massive profit.

An American in Paris simultaneously bears the signatures of both Gene Kelly and Vincente Minnelli, but the movie is one of the best examples of the luscious, almost hysterically vibrant aesthetic of Minnelli in particular. The climactic 16-minute ballet sequence, titled "The American in Paris," is a great representative example of the director's baroque style. Minnelli always maintained a clear divide between the "ordinary" world of the everyday and the fantastical dream world that surfaces through his musical numbers, and this is on full display in the film. The plot is also pure Minnelli; as the title indicates, Kelly stars as Jerry, an American ex-soldier who moves to Paris in order to become a painter. While there, he meets and falls in love with Lise (played by Leslie Caron.)

Kelly in *An American in Paris*

While Vincente Minnelli was responsible for the stunning visuals of *An American in Paris*, it is Kelly who must be credited for the virtuoso dance routines. The eponymous ballet sequence is a highlight of Kelly's career, and according to Beth Genne, film ballets became quite popular at MGM in the wake of the film's success. Moreover, as Emanuel Levy argues, *An American in Paris* captures the visual and acoustic pleasure that is intrinsic to the musical: "More than anything else, An American in Paris is a musical about visual pleasure, in which the protagonist creates through song and dance his own live and lively audience of children on the street, patrons of fancy cafes, and his own pals. It's also a movie about rhythm, as the American ex-G.I. makes clear when he sings "I Got Rhythm," and it's a stylized spectacle of and about Paris, a city whose long history and various cityscapes offer Jerry (and Minnelli) the subject and inspiration for his paintings." (406).

As this description suggests, *An American in Paris* transforms everyday reality into a world filled with dramatic visual displays and joyous rhythm. These qualities manifest just as strongly in Kelly's next picture, *Singin' in the Rain*, the most famous film of Kelly's career. It is virtually synonymous with the genre, and the title song holds a special place within American culture.

Where *An American in Paris* is a tribute to Paris's ability to inspire one's artistic sensibility, *Singin' in the Rain* focuses on the motion picture industry, the most quintessentially American art form. Kelly plays a film actor during the moment in which Hollywood was just beginning to transfer to synchronized sound, and his co-star, Lina Lamont (played by Jean Hagen), possesses a shrill voice that requires another actress, Kathy Selden (played by Debbie Reynolds), to dub her lines. This becomes problematic when they decide to adapt their hit film, The Dueling Cavalier, into a musical (titled The Dancing Cavalier), because Lina can no longer convincingly have Kathy dub her lines. Eventually, her voice is exposed, and it is revealed that her voice is produced by another actress.

Singin' in the Rain is amazing on multiple levels. First, the musical numbers are expertly choreographed; as with *On the Town*, Stanley Donen serves as co-choreographer and co-director, and sequences such as "Singin' in the Rain," "Moses Supposes," "You are My Lucky Star" and "Good Morning" are all iconic. If *Singin' in the Rain* qualifies as a masterpiece, though, it is also because it contains a more absorbing plot than most other musicals. Many films of the genre contain plots that essentially act as filler in between the singing and dancing sequences, but *Singin' in the Rain* boasts a narrative that is entertaining in its own right and a commentary on cinema during the formative years of the sound era. The plot is a foremost example of what Jane Feuer has referred to as "conservative reflexivity," in which the plot refers to the process of performing in order to ultimately affirm the joys of live entertainment. This can be seen in *Singin' in the Rain* through the fact that the movie addresses the industrial challenges that Hollywood faced at the advent of the sound era, only to end with a triumphant shot of Kathy and Don in front of a billboard advertising their next film. Thus, the movie succeeds not only on the strength of its musical numbers and plot but also because it stands as a testament to the delights of American entertainment.

Kelly in *Singin' in the Rain*

Another reason that *Singin' in the Rain* is so important to the genre is that it combines a number of motifs associated with the genre. In his analysis of the genre, Rick Altman delineates three categories: the show musical, the fairy tale musical, and the folk musical. In the show musical, the narrative centers on the production of a show within the show, the production of which culminates in a performance at the film's conclusion. Meanwhile, in the fairy tale musical, the dance sequences transform the characters to a fantasy space in which the man and woman preside over a sort of magical kingdom, a category best exemplified in the films of Fred Astaire and Ginger Rogers. Finally, in the folk musical, the characters are everyday folk who break into song in order to express their unbounded emotion. In *Singin' in the Rain*, viewers can see elements of both the show musical and the folk musical. The production qualifies the movie as a show musical, yet the many sequences off the film set, including the musical number that gives the film its title, are key examples of the folk musical category. Thus, the movie is not only one of the most entertaining musicals ever made but a worthy reference into the most salient components of the genre as a whole.

Singin' in the Rain was released on January 1, 1952, but immediately before it came out, Kelly made a decision that would dramatically alter the trajectory of his career. Late in 1951, he signed with MGM to a contract that stipulated that he make three films in Europe over the course of the next 19 months. The rationale behind this was that the studio had money tied up in Europe, and

Kelly stood to benefit from the tax benefits associated with working overseas. However, the project was disastrous, and only one of the films Kelly made there, *Invitation to the Dance*, was actually a musical. Furthermore, *Invitation to the Dance* experienced substantial delays and was not actually released until 1956, ultimately failing miserably. Making matters worse was that when Gene returned to America in 1953, the musical was beginning to feel the threat of television. MGM opted to cut the budget of *Brigadoon* (1954), his first film after returning, and the movie was not successful, exacerbating his increasingly bitter relations with the studio he had remained with his entire career.

Looking back at Gene Kelly's career, it was not inevitable that his career would decline during the 1950s. There were successful musicals released during the decade, and two of them, *Guys and Dolls* (1955) and *Pal Joey* (1957), drew interest from Kelly, but these films were not produced by MGM and the studio refused to loan him. Disgusted, Kelly finally negotiated an end to his contract after agreeing to appear in three more films with them, but those pictures - *It's Always Fair Weather* (1956), *Les Girls* (1957), and *The Happy Road* (1957) - had varying degrees of success. None of those movies were major successes, and by the end of 1957, Kelly was gone from the studio and ready to explore new avenues not only as an actor but also a producer and director.

Even if Gene's final films with MGM were unremarkable, the production history of *It's Always Fair Weather* deserves mention, because Kelly had long been a fervent member of the Democratic Party who opposed the House Un-American American Committee. This was not the first time in which he had made his political and religious views known; he had also become politically involved in 1939, when he broke away from the Roman Catholic Church in protest of their support of Francisco Franco and disregard for the plight of the poor. In 1955, his wife was accused of being a Communist sympathizer, leading United Artists to remove her from the starring role of *Marty*, but Kelly recognized that MGM maintained close ties with United Artists, so he removed himself from the production of *It's Always Fair Weather* until United Artists gave Kelly's wife her part once again. This episode highlights how even though Gene shied away from identifying himself with the Communist Party, he refused to cave in to the scare tactics adopted throughout Hollywood during the height of the Red Scare.

Kelly's professional troubles were also compounded by the collapse of his marriage with Betsy Blair. The couple divorced in 1957, and it would be three years before he would remarry, this time to Jeanne Coyne in 1960. The story behind his relationship with Coyne is interesting as well, because she was a choreographic assistant who had previously been married to Kelly's close friend, Stanley Donen. Kelly seemed to confirm the rumors that he was having an affair with Donen's wife, while Donen was in love with Kelly's wife Betsy at the same time: "Jeannie's marriage to Stanley was doomed from the start. Because every time Stanley looked at Jeannie, he saw Betsy, whom he loved; and every time Jeannie looked at Stanley, I guess she saw me. One way or another it was all pretty incestuous." Gene and Coyne remained happily married until Jeanne's death in 1973, and they had two children together: a son (Timothy in 1962) and a daughter (Bridget 1964).

Kelly and Coyne

Chapter 6: Late Career and Retirement

"I'll never starve." – Gene Kelly

When Gene Kelly left MGM in 1957, his career took a new direction of sorts, now focused more on producing and directing than on acting. He also returned to the theater, and his first post-MGM venture involved directing the Rodgers and Hammerstein musical *Flower Drum Song* (1958). Then, in 1960, he created a ballet, *Pas de Dieux*, for the Paris Opera and Opera-Comique (Kelly was fluent in French so there was no linguistic barrier). Kelly also explored television, and in 1962 and 1963 he starred as Father Chuck O'Malley in the program *Going My Way*. Kelly signed with Universal in 1963, but nothing materialized, and even though he continued to act in movies during the decade, not all of these late films were musicals.

In 1960, Kelly acted in *Inherit the Wind*, playing a newspaper reporter assigned to cover a case in which a teacher stands on trial for teaching the theory of evolution. The movie was not particularly successful, and Kelly continued to focus more closely on the production end. One of his grander efforts of the decade was *Gigot* (1962), a film he directed in Paris, but to his dismay, Seven Arts Productions made substantial editing cuts and the movie failed at the box office. Kelly appeared as himself in the Marilyn Monroe-headed musical comedy *Let's Make Love* (1960), and had a relatively minor role in the hit comedy *What a Way to Go* (1964), but it was clear by now that his career was well into its decline. A late career highlight came when Kelly appeared in the acclaimed French musical *Les Demoiselles de Roquefort* (1966), but his reluctance to veer far from Hollywood precluded further projects overseas.

Kelly in the trailer for *Inherit the Wind*

In 1965, Gene signed with Fox, but once again he found it difficult to agree on any projects, and the films he did make for the studio are mostly forgettable. Of these, the best came in 1967, when he directed Walter Matthau in the comedy *A Guide for the Married Man*, a film that was far from a masterpiece but was popular with American viewers. Less successful were Kelly's subsequent directorial efforts, which included *Hello, Dolly* (1969) and the western picture *The Cheyenne Social Club* (1970), both of which were flops. Gene Kelly's major strength had always lay in his ability to direct and choreograph himself, so it should come as no surprise that his late-career films performed so poorly. He certainly did better when he starred in the three *That's Entertainment* films, a series of quasi-documentaries commemorating the landmark films of MGM. In the first and second movies, he appears alongside Fred Astaire, offering the rare opportunity to witness the two legends together.

During the 1970s, Gene also appeared as himself on several television programs, but he would not appear in a series again until *North and South* (1985) and *Sins* (1986). In 1980, he made the surprising decision to act in the musical *Xanadu* (1980), which also starred Michael Beck and Olivia Newton-John, but that unpopular movie marked the last time Kelly acted in a film. The final movie in which he was involved was the animated picture *Cats Don't Dance* (1997), which he was involved in throughout parts of 1994.

While his career clearly suffered, his personal life was more joyous. In 1990, he married his third wife, Patricia Ward, and he remained married for the rest of his life. However, as the 1990s progressed, Kelly began to suffer from strokes. The first of these occurred in July 1994, necessitating a hospital stay of seven weeks, and an additional stroke came the next year, leaving him bedridden. Gene Kelly passed away on February 2, 1996, at the age of 83, and in an unconventional decision, he arranged for his body to be cremated, thus forgoing a funeral or other traditional burial service.

In all, Gene Kelly's film career spanned several decades and resulted in dozens of films, but he will forever be remembered for the extraordinary run of success he experienced from 1945-1952, from *Anchors Aweigh* through *Singin' in the Rain*. During this stretch, he effectively achieved his goal of demonstrating that the hero of the film musical could be a virile, overtly masculine figure who captured the viewers' attention as much or more than his female co-star. Fred Astaire had captured viewers' hearts with his graceful, intricately choreographed routines with Ginger Rogers, but Kelly broke away from Astaire's more dandified image, starting a trend of portraying bold masculinity that would be used by subsequent stars like Marlon Brando, Kirk Douglas, and other actors of the late 1940s and 1950s. This boldness extended beyond the screen as well; the conservative Astaire was reticent to publicly take a political stand, but Kelly was unafraid to let his liberal views be known. More than anything else, while there is no questioning Fred Astaire's rightful place in the history of Hollywood entertainment, it must be said that Kelly's more down-to-earth portrayal took the image of the film musical hero and made it more accessible to an American audience.

As successful as Kelly was, it is also telling that his first movie was not even released until 1942, when he was 30. As a result, ironically, he was by no means destined to become an actor, and in fact he had a fairly long and successful career on Broadway during the 1930s and even the vaudeville stage during the prior decade. Since his acting career encompasses many stages, it's a valuable resource through which to chart the evolution of American entertainment in the 20th century, from vaudeville to Broadway to the height of the Hollywood musical to the unfortunate demise of the musical in the late 1950s and early 1960s. If the final decades of Kelly's career were filled with conflict and unfulfilled promise, however, this should not obscure the overwhelming triumphs he experienced after returning from World War II. Kelly was very much his mother's son, as he inherited her hardworking ethos and satisfied her dream to have a son make it big as a musical entertainer. After all, as sad as the 1950s and 1960s were for Kelly, the enduring images of him will always be as the American in Paris or the joyous gentleman thrilled to be singin' in the rain.

Bibliography

Altman, Rick. The American Film Musical. Bloomington: Indiana University Press, 1989.

Print.

Astaire, Fred. Steps in Time: An Autobiography. New York: HarperCollins, 2008. Print.

Cohan, Steven. "Dancing with Balls in the 1940s: Sissies, Sailors and the Camp Masculinity of Gene Kelly." The Trouble with Men: Masculinities in European and Hollywood Cinema. Eds. Phil Powrie, Ann Davies, and Bruce Babington. London, United Kingdom: Wallflower Press, 2004. 18-33. Print.

Cullen, Frank. Vaudeville, Old & New: An Encyclopedia of Variety Performers in America. London, United Kingdom: Routledge, 2006. Print.

Farber, Manny. Farber on Film. New York: Library of America, 2009. Print.

Feuer, Jane. The Hollywood Musical. Bloomington: Indiana University Press, 1993. Print.

Genne, Beth. "Vincente Minnelli and the Film Ballet." Vincene Minnelli: The Art of Entertainment. Ed. Joe McElhaney. Detroit: Wayne State University Press, 2009. 229-251. Print.

Green, Stanley. Hollywood Musicals Year by Year. Milwaukee: Hal Leonard Corporation, 1999. Print.

Hirschhorn, Clive. Gene Kelly: A Biography. Chicago: Henry Regenry Company, 1975. Print.

Hischak, Thomas S., ed. The Rodgers and Hammerstein Encyclopedia. Westport: Greenwood, 2007. Print.

Levy, Emanuel. Vincente Minnelli: Hollywood's Dark Dreamer. New York: St. Martin's Press, 2009. Print.

Paris, James Robert, and Michael R. Pitts. Hollywood Songsters: Garland to O'Conner. London, United Kingdom: Routledge, 2003. Print.

Thomas, Tony. The Films of Gene Kelly: Song and Dance Man. New York: Citadel Press, 1974. Print.

Yudkoff, Alvin. Gene Kelly: A Life of Dance and Dreams. New York: Back Stage Books, 1999. Print.

Printed in Great Britain
by Amazon

21372551R00020

A Quick Guide to Ranks of the British Army

Don Benson Books

About the Author

Don Benson was born and raised in the North East of England. In his professional life he has worked in and alongside a number of museums and historical associations, re-enactment groups and primary schools. He is also an instructor in the cadet forces. From these he has a wealth of experience and knowledge which he draws on when creating his books.

You can read more about the author here-
https://don-benson.com/

Chapter 1

Since its formation in 1660 the British Army has developed and adapted a structure of rank to ensure flexibility and efficiency on the battlefield. Each rank has a set responsibility and the necessary training and experience to be able to take over the role of the rank above them. Some ranks that you may be familiar with will have been retired whilst others have had their names changed or new ranks added. With such a long history and multiple refinements the modern British Army is a well led, experienced and fearsome fighting force.

We must also understand when discussing ranks that some named roles are not ranks but are indeed appointments. An appointment may for example be as an adjutant. An adjutant works as an administrative aid to a senior officer. Usually the appointment of adjutant would be held by a captain or a major. In this way the rank is captain or major and the appointment is as an adjutant.

Ranks can be separated into two main groups.
1. Commissioned ranks. A commissioned rank is any officer that has passed their basic training and officer cadet course.
2. Other ranks. (OR's) Often named incorrectly as ordinary ranks, other ranks refers to any ranks which does not hold a commission from the crown.

Other Ranks include non-commissioned officers and warrant officers. Although these grades contain the word officer in their title they are not the same as commissioned officers.

NATO codes exist for each rank. These are marked as either OR-* for other ranks or OF-* for commissioned ranks. NATO codes exist due to the close working relationship between NATO countries and allows for commands to be transferred easily. NATO codes help militaries work together by clearly setting out seniority for international military exercises or interventions.

The current professional head of the army is The Chief of the General Staff (CGS) General Sir Mark Carleton-Smith. The CGS reports to the Chief of the Defence Staff (CDS) Admiral Sir Tony Radakin RN. The CDS is the most senior uniformed advisor the the government in military matters. The head of the armed forces in Queen Elizabeth II, it is to the Queen that members of the armed forces swear allegiance.

We will now begin looking at the ranks from the bottom up, beginning with the most junior.

Private (Pte) (OR-1 OR-2)
No badge of rank
A private is the most junior soldier in the British Army and is the rank all soldiers are given once

they have completed their phase one training. Depending on the regiment the soldier is serving in their rank may be an equivalent of private. These can include;

Trooper(Tpr)- Most cavalry regiments use the rank of trooper for their most junior soldiers.

Signaller(Sig)- A signaller serves in the Royal Corps of Signals.

Gunner(Gnr)- Soldiers serving in the Royal Artillery will pass out with the rank of gunner after basic training.

Guardsman(Gdsm)- Guards regiments such as the Grenadier and Coldstream Guards use the rank of guardsman in place of private.

Rifleman(Rfn)- The Rifles use the rank of Rifleman.

Kingsman(Kgn)- This rank exists only as part of the Duke of Lancaster's Regiment.

Fusilier(Fus)- Soldiers of the Royal Regiment of Fusiliers carry this rank.

Sapper(Spr)- Royal Engineers.

Airtrooper(AirTpr)- Army Air Corps

Craftsman(Cfn)- Royal Electrical and Mechanical Engineers.

Highlander(Hldr)- Highland Regiments.

Ranger(Rgr)- Royal Irish Regiment.

Musicians and band members also have distinguished ranks.

Drummer(Dmr), Trumpeter(Tptr), Piper(Ppr), Bandsman(Former rank) Bdsm), Musician(Musn) and Bugler(Bgr).

These ranks are not usually put in charge of groups of soldiers unless as part of an exercise or in an emergency.

Chapter 2

NCO's

The following ranks are the ranks of Non Commissioned Officers also known as NCO's. NCO's are experienced soldiers that have a few years of service behind them. NCO's are trained to command small groups of soldiers or to handle administrative and welfare tasks. NCO training courses expand on the basic training all soldiers receive but add a special emphasis on map work and navigation, leadership, military law, and battle tactics. Some NCO courses, especially those in trade branches of the armed forces, will focus on the specific trade of the prospective NCO and will link closely to their phase 2 training.

The NCO's are often referred to as the backbone of the army, a truth widely recognised in most modern armed forces. Historically, NCO's were entrusted with tasks that would not or could not be entrusted to officers. In the Royal Navy these included the specialised roles of Gunner, Carpenter and Bosun. In the British Army roles such as Colour Sergeants came about with tough experienced sergeants entrusted with the defence of a regiment's colours or standards, the rallypoint in battles and the regimental pride. In the Royal Air Force a great deal of NCO's flew aircraft, served as navigators, flight engineers,wireless operators, and air gunners. They also served capably on the ground as armourers, fitters and in control rooms.

Many young officers owe their survival and advancement through the ranks to the NCO's around them.

Modern militaries that have a weak, or indeed, non-existent NCO cadre, often struggle with undertaking effective military operations. NCO's take on roles which allow officers to focus on decision making and leadership. Without the capability of those men and women officers workload is doubled at minimum and the ability to make rapid decisions on the ground is severely impacted.

Lance-corporal or equivalent (L/Cpl) (OR-3)
One chevron.

This is the most junior NCO rank. A lance corporal is second in command of a section and works under the command of a corporal. Specialist positions such as drivers or mortarmen may be promoted to lance corporal on completion of phase two training. The most recent Victoria Cross recipient was Lance Corporal (now sergeant) Joshua Leaky of the 1st Battalion the Parachute Regiment who during a joint US UK patrol rendered first aid to a USMC captain and then ran through enemy fire multiple times to man a machinegun, site a second machinegun and return fire to the enemy. THE MOD summary of his actions are thus; Under fire yet undeterred by the very clear and present danger, Lance Corporal Leakey ran across the exposed slope of the hill three times to initiate casualty evacuation, re-site machine guns and return fire. His actions proved the turning point, inspiring his comrades to fight back with renewed ferocity. Displaying gritty leadership well above that expected of his rank, Lance Corporal Leakey's actions singlehandedly regained the initiative and prevented considerable loss of life.

Corporal or equivalent (Cpl) (OR-4)
Two chevrons.
A corporal is an experienced soldier in charge of an infantry section or tank. Corporals are usually in charge of groups of around seven to twelve soldiers or can command specialist teams such as a mortar team, machine gun team or vehicle. Corporals are also part of training teams for military instruction centres and training camps such as ITC Catterick. In the guards division a corporal is known by the rank lance-sergeant and wears three chevrons instead of two. To distinguish between a lance-sergeant and full sergeant the chevrons are white rather than gold. Promotion to corporal can follow after 6-8 years service but can occur sooner.

Sergeant or equivalent (Sgt) (OR-5 OR-6)
Three chevrons.
A sergeant is a senior enlisted soldier that has a wealth of experience. Not many junior officers dismiss a sergeant's advice and come through unscathed. A sergeant is typically second in command of a platoon but can also lead a section or team similar to a corporal. Sergeant's will

sometimes lead platoons themselves but this has become a rarity. Sergeants are often a key link between commissioned officers and the enlisted men, they take an active role in the training of new soldiers, administration duties, welfare and specialised roles. Note that the household cavalry does not use the rank sergeant but Corporal of Horse. This is due to the rank of sergeant stemming from the word 'servant' historically a cavalry regiment was staffed by gentlemen, never a servant. Promotion to sergeant typically takes place after 10-12 years of service.

In The Rifles sergeant is spelt with a j, as in Serjeant. This is a more archaic spelling and is one of the traditions that has continued despite the original regiment that did this being merged with many others.

Staff sergeant/colour sergeant (S/Sgt//C/Sgt or equivalent (OR-7)

Three chevrons below a crown.

Staff sergeant's are the last enlisted NCO rank and usually fulfill a very specific role. Quartermaster roles are often filled by staff sergeants and are known as CQMS(Company Quatermaster Sergeant) or SQMS (Squadron Quartermaster Sergeant). The correct form of address for a staff/colour sergeant is staff/colour sergeant or colour/staff. Promotion to staff sergeant takes place after a few years as a sergeant.

Chapter 4

Warrant Officers

A warrant officer is technically neither a Non Commissioned Officer nor a Commissioned Officer but is usually considered an NCO. A Warrant Officer's authority is granted through a Royal Warrant which is a distinct class of its own. The term Warrant Officer originates with the Royal Navy when specialised roles such as carpenter, boatswain (bosun) and gunner where appointed via a royal warrant rather than a commission. Upon reaching the rank of warrant officer a person can apply for a late entry (LE) commission. This allows them to enter officer training upon the completion of which they will automatically be promoted to full lieutenant. In some cases sergeants can be selected for LE commissions but this has fallen out of practice.

Warrant Officer Class 2 (WO2) (OR-8)

Crown sometimes surrounded by a wreath. Worn on the forearm when wearing No.2 service dress. A WO2 is a senior soldier who can hold a number of roles but is best known as being a Company Sergeant Major (CSM) or Squadron Sergeant Major (SSM). A WO2 can also hold roles such as Sergeant Major of Signals, Sergeant Major of Transport or Sergeant Major or Quartermaster Sergeant Instructor. WO2's are usually in charge of administration, welfare and training of groups up to and including the company or half battalion level.

A notable WO2 was Stan Hollis who served in the 6th Battalion The Green Howards(currently part of The Yorkshire Regiment) who was the only soldier awarded the Victoria Cross on D-day for his actions in taking enemy positions virtually single handed and in rescuing his men under fire. Not your typical hero, Hollis was neither handsome nor a particularly good soldier. At one time he threw a grenade which failed to explode because he had forgotten to pull the pin. Nevertheless, his actions, borne from the desire to keep his men safe, are the same instincts that all Warrant Officers share.

Warrant Officer Class 1 (WO1) (OR-9)
Coat of Arms, sometimes surrounded by a wreath. Worn on the forearm when wearing No.2 service dress.
A WO1 is usually appointed to oversee specialised roles in a technical and non-combat capacity. A WO1 can also be appointed as a Regimental Sergeant Major (RSM). A WO1 is usually in charge of discipline, ammunition resupply and the handling of prisoners of war. WO1's have a long history of being as fearsome in combat as on the parade ground.

There are distinct appointments which can make a WO1 senior to another WO1. These are in order of seniority lowest to highest.

1. Conductor. Royal Logistics Corps.

2. Royal Artillery Sergeant Major. Royal Artillery.
3. Academy Sergeant Major. Royal Military Academy Sandhurst.
4. Garrison Sergeant Major. London District.
5. Army Sergeant Major. The most senior warrant officer in the British Army.

WO1's are promoted after 18 years of outstanding service. This is often the aspiration for many career soldiers. A WO1, also sometimes known as 'The Badge' has been a feared and respected member of any unit for as long as the position has existed. Acting as a battalion commander's right hand man the WO1 is an important part of any command structure.

Stories abound of junior officers being told to do whatever the RSM tells them to do. One story I was told was of an RSM who took over the guard duty for a sergeant whose wife was in the process of giving birth. The RSM had his men fallen in at 3 o'clock ready for the officer to come and inspect them. At one minute past the hour he sent one of the men to fetch the officer. A few minutes later the man returned, and rather pale faced addressed the Sergeant-Major, "I'm sorry sir, but ermmmm…Mr Smith says he will come when he is ready and not before."

The RSM ordered the guard to fix bayonets and arrested the officer for dereliction of duty. The colonel told the officer, when he was marched in, to do exactly as the RSM tells him and both of their lives would be simpler.

I cannot remember the name of the RSM nor officer but believe that the regiment in question was the Shropshires.

Another story was of a Parachute regiment RSM who, whilst pace sticking, dropped his stick which he then loudly and firmly ordered to stand up whilst on parade.

Another during the Second World War of a church parade where a soldier neglected to remove his headdress as he entered church. The RSM bawled out, and I quote exactly, "Remove your effing headdress, you are in a church you c***!"

Chapter 5
Commissioned Ranks
A commissioned officer is a person who holds a Royal Commision. Historically, an individual that held a royal commission was a member of the aristocracy, often with no military skills or experience. From the age of thirteen a well-to-do boy could expect a commission as a junior officer in his fathers or uncles regiment or be sponsored to one with a friend of the family. Making up for a lack of military skills with the ability to read, a good knowledge of horses and familial connections these young officers were often very poor at their work. The practice of buying and selling commissions was also widespread before Wellington did away with the practice. Any person could purchase for themselves a commission as an officer, provided they could read and could afford it. This caused problems as wealthy men could buy their way up to the rank of lieutenant-colonel whilst men with skill but no funds were stuck as subalterns all their lives. Luckily, tough NCO's acted as the backbone of the army and a good number of the young gentlemen went on to become famous soldiers whose names echo across battlefields today. Names such as Arthur Wellesley, the Duke of Wellington, John Churchill, Duke of Marlborough, Sir Colin Campbell and Sir John Moore.

The Great War changed the officer cadre forever. During one period on the western front a junior officer's life expectancy was two weeks. Because of the horrendous cost in officers, more and more men from humble backgrounds earned commissions, a feat repeated in the Second World War. A great many unlikely characters became officers, those from poor backgrounds often showed they had the grit and quick mind necessary to lead.

Currently commissioned officers in the armed forces undergo the same basic training as enlisted men, with an extended course to teach leadership, welfare, personnel management, military law, tactical and strategic leadership and military history.

Officer Cadet (OCdt) OF(D)

Single White Strip

An officer cadet is a trainee officer. They are marked by a single white stripe on their rank slide. An officer cadet may attend University Officer Training or be enrolled at a military college such as Sandhurst. Officer cadets have no formal command obligations but will be given tasks to complete as a platoon leader such as leading the other cadets on a night patrol or constructing and explaining sand tables.

Second Lieutenant or equivalent (2Lt/2ndLt) (OF-1)

A single pip/ star.

This is the most junior commissioned rank in the British army and is awarded immediately after completing officer training. In command of a troop or platoon of around thirty soldiers. The responsibilities of a platoon leader focus on the welfare and training of 30 soldiers. Junior officers should always listen to the advice of their platoon sergeant who is usually their senior in both experience and years. Officers are called sir by those junior to them and Mr (Name)or Miss (Name) by those senior. Lieutenant comes from the words for place holder as a lieutenant was the placeholder for their company when battles were still fought by lines of infantry with muskets. They were also the placeholder for their captain if he was unable to command.

Lieutenant or equivalent (Lt) (OF-1)
Two pips/stars, one above the other.
After a period of time as a second lieutenant, usually two years or less, an officer can expect promotion to lieutenant. Still a subaltern the change in role from second lieutenant to lieutenant is fairly minor, though additional training opportunities and a small bump in pay is available alongside a few additional responsibilities.

Captain (Cpt/Capt) (OF-2)
Three pips/stars, in a vertical line.
A captain can command a company of between 50 to 120 soldiers and can also serve in special appointments such as liaison, adjutant or as a company/squadron/battery commander though this has become more the role of a major. Captain's

often command more than a platoon but less than a company. Promotion to captain can follow after three years of commissioned service. Captain Nolan of Charge of The Light Brigade fame held this rank.

Major (Maj) (OF-3)
Crown without a wreath. Worn on the epaulette of No.2 service dress rather than on the wrist as a warrant officer would.

Majors tend to command companies,squadrons or batteries rather than captains as would have been done originally. A major is a fairly senior rank within a battalion and is responsible for around 120-200 soldiers. They work closely with warrant officers to ensure their soldiers are taken care of. Majors can be appointed to run training schools, military outposts and as second in command of a battalion. Promotion to major can happen after 8-10 years in the army. Major John Howard DSO was in command of the glider bourne assault that captured the Caen Canal as part of the D-Day operations.

Lieutenant-colonel (Lt Col) (OF-4)
A crown above a star.

A Lieutenant-colonel is often referred to simply as colonel and is in command of an infantry battalion, artillery regiment or cavalry regiment. Commanding 650+ soldiers the role of a lieutenant-colonel is very demanding. A colonel will work closely with the RSM and his majors to ensure his command is running effectively. A Lt-col is the last rank you would reasonably expect to see serving on the frontline though usually they will spend their time in command and control situations rather than in the firefight. There is no expected promotion time to lieutenant-colonel as there are few positions for an awful lot of applicants, therefore only those who are excellent soldiers or have a distinguished record are promoted to lieutenant-colonel. Even so a great many excellent majors never see their opportunity to command a battalion. A Colonel should not be confused with a Colonel of the Regiment who is usually a retired general who protects the interests of the regiment and represents them at formal functions.

Colonel H Jones of the parachute regiment was killed in action during the Falklands War. His actions, although undoubtedly heroic, have received criticism from some areas due to the belief that his role was to command rather than to fight on the front line.

Another notable Lieutenant-Colonel was John Frost, also of the parachute regiment that fought during the battle of Arnhem.

Colonel (Col) (OF-5)
A crown above two pips.
Colonel is the fist staff rank, with responsibilities being to the administration of a brigade or division. They may also command units larger than a battalion but smaller than a brigade. A colonel can also be placed in command of military installations such as a field hospital. Colonels will not spend

anytime on the front line as their role is key in the organisation of their parent unit. Colonels can also be assigned as military attaches or advisors.

Brigadier (Brig) (OF-6)

A triangle of three pips surmounted by a crown. A brigadier commands a brigade or holds staff appointments, usually in the organisation and administration of a division. Brigadiers, along with colonels can serve as military attaches and advisors or operate with an individual command. Originally the rank of brigadier was brigadier general and was the most junior general officer rank, this was changed in the 1920's ro revert to field officer rank.

Major General (Maj Gen) (OF-7)

Crossed sword(sabre) and baton beneath a pip. A Major General typically commands a division of mixed forces to support one another and act independently. This is the most junior general rank and is often simply known as general.

Lieutenant General (Lt Gen) (OF-8)

Crossed sword(sabre) and baton beneath a crown. A Lieutenant General is usually found in command of a corps (pronounced core) or holds a senior staff appointment. Lieutenant generals play an important role in planning for future conflicts, overseeing the strategic role of the army and preserving the golden thread that connects the history of the army to its future.

General (Gen) (OF-9)

Crossed sword(sabre) and baton beneath a pip beneath a crown. Generals usually command an army or army group. This is the highest granted rank in the British army. Generals will often lead the strategic view of the army and will spend a lot of time in communication with the government to ensure the armed forces are capable and up to date. Generals wield an awesome amount of power both militarily and politically within the army.

Field Marshall (FM) (OF-10)

Two crossed batons surrounded by a wreath beneath a crown.

Currently the rank of field marshall is an honorary one only as no person is currently promoted to this rank during peacetime. Only 141 people have ever held the rank of FM in the British Army. Sir Peter Inge was the last active officer to be promoted to the rank in 1994, though his successor was promoted to FM as an honorary rank.

A notable holder of this post was Sir Arthur Wellesley, The Duke of Wellington.

The rank of Field Marshall is a less important rank than it was in 1815. Back then a field marshall commanded most of his troops in line of sight or by messenger on a fast horse. Now, a field marshall would be sending orders too far from the situation in country to be aware of operational needs.

Field Marshal Bernard Montgomery is possibly one of the best remembered field marshals of recent times for his role in WW2 especially during the North African campaign. Despite falling out with many other allied officers he was able to carry off a number of excellent strategies. Monty, as he was known to his men, was the mind behind the disastrous Market Garden operation during which the Allies attempted to capture key bridges in Holland in order to outflank the German military and bring the war to a quicker end. Unfortunately, due to serious strategic oversight and lack of coordination between the Army and RAF the British and Polish airborne forces suffered serious losses with a great many of them being killed or captured in Arnhem.

More can be read about the Polish contribution to Market Garden here:
http://www.polandinexile.com/marketgarden.htm

Chapter 6

The regulations on how ranks should be worn have changed drastically over the centuries that the British army has evolved. At first ranks would be marked by knots of silver or gold braiding on the shoulder of a coat and the piping along the edge of a coat and hat. Usually the more silver or gold on your uniform the higher rank you were. The Royal Navy was the first service to adopt the epaulette as an official part of their uniform in 1795, however many regiments in the army formed their own rank and ways of displaying them, before 1767 there was no rank insignia at all for field marshals or general officers. In 1791 officers were ordered to wear different epaulettes and shoulder wings to distinguish between different regimental officers (from ensign to lieutenant-colonel). It was not until 1810 that badges of rank were adopted for general officer ranks. Foot Guards Regiments were not issued badges of rank for officers until 1815. Foot Guards officers were not equal to those in line regiments, for example Captains of the Guards were equal to line regiments Lieutenant-Colonels, Lieutenants were equivalent with Majors and Ensigns (Second lieutenants in modern lingo) were equal to Captains of the line.

It was not until 1829 that badges of rank were standardised across the army.

In 1855 at the end of the Crimean War the army abolished all wing and epaulette rank badges and replaced them with collar badges. This was the first time that the broad spectrum of the army had the same badges of rank worn in the same way. The army changed its mind again in 1880 and changed badges or rank to the shoulder. This rank structure is similar to the modern although a second lieutenant wore no device, a lieutenant wore a single pip and a captain two. This was changed to the modern system in 1902 with officers below general rank wearing their rank on the cuff.

Before the beginning of the First World War officers began wearing their badges of rank on the cuff, rather than on the shoulder. Although this made it easier for others to see the rank it also made it easier for German snipers to pick out officers and ranks quickly returned to the shoulder. This was not officially sanctioned until 1917 as optional then made a permanent change in 1920. During this time many officers and regiments still made their own judgements on how ranks should be worn and many odd spacings of badge of rank can be seen. Full standardisation of the British Army would not take place until post World War Two.

In modern times rank is most often worn in the centre of the chest by all ranks when wearing a working uniform. When wearing more formal uniform such as for parades ranks are worn as stated in each section.

Defunct Ranks

Bandsman - replaced my musician.

Captain-General - ~1400-~1700 roughly equal in rank to a General or Field Marshall in historical armies. This rank fell out of use in the early to mid 1700's. This rank is still held by the head of The Honourable Artillery Company, the senior officer for The Royal Company of Archers. The Colonel in Chief of the Royal Marines and Colonel in Chief of the Royal Regiment of Artillery hold the rank of Captain General. None of these ranks are equal to a modern General and are mostly ceremonial.

Captain-lieutenant - This rank was held by the lieutenant of the first company of the regiment. When promoted to full captain the time spent as lieutenant-captain was considered time served as captain.

Sergeant-Major General - The original name for Major General.

Ensign- Replaced in 1871 by the rank Second Lieutenant. Ensigns were often as young as thirteen or fourteen. The two most senior ensigns carried the regimental colours. In some Guards regiments the rank of Ensign is still used to refer to Second Lieutenants.

Cornet- Replaced by Second Lieutenant in 1871. The cavalry equivalent to an Ensign. The Blues and

Royals and Queens Royal Hussars still use this rank to refer to Second Lieutenants.

The following ranks are specialist ranks that have fallen out of use. This is not a comprehensive list as some ranks were created and fell out of use with little record of them or were only used in a particular regiment.

Platoon Sergeant Major, Saddler, Wheelwright, Corporal-Sergeant, Dresser, Smith/Blacksmith, Farrier Sergeant, Tailor, Clerk, Writer, Cook, Senior Cook, Saddlemaker, Leatherworker, Artificer, Ordnancier, Mortarman, Paymaster Sergeant, Corporal-Major.

Many ranks have odd spellings especially in records before 1915. This is due to localised spellings and regimental oddities. The rank of Sergeant for examples has been spelt as Sergeant, Sargent, Sirgent, Serjeant, Siregent, Servant, Sirevent and Sergent. This is due in part to the accents of those writing the records and due to the poor education many soldiers experienced, especially before the Education Act of 1880 which made school compulsory for children between the ages of five and ten, though this was not rigorously enforced.

More can be read about ranks of the British Army here: https://www.army.mod.uk/who-we-are/our-people/ranks/

<u>mentioned in the acknowledgements section.</u>

Printed in Great Britain
by Amazon

21373092R00020